GRETTA BERRY

You Are What You Say

How Your Words Shape Your World

Contents

1

Introduction

Have you ever wondered why you say some of the things you say? Have you paid any attention to what you say about yourself? Or what you say about others, whether casually or repeating something you've heard someone else say? I have recently noticed more and more what people say about themselves. The question enters my mind, "Do they think about themselves that way? Do they honestly feel that way about themselves?" The more I hear what people say about themselves, the more I realize how powerful those words are. Have you ever noticed a mom calling a child bad for years and then wondered why the child becomes a terror as they get older? Do you think it's because she told the child they were bad since they were a toddler? What else should you expect the child to be? Words are extremely powerful and in this book, I hope to help you shift your words and thoughts about yourself and those around you from negative words to more positive words. It is easy to simply say what you've heard others say and not think anything of it, but wouldn't it be great to move from the ways of the past and transform the future?

2

What to Expect

The purpose of this book is to help bring awareness to what you say, what you think, what you allow to be said about you, and what you agree with that is said to you. It is to help bring your attention to positive or negative thoughts and words. By the end of this book, I hope that you will be more cognizant of your words said to yourself, your spouse, and your children. I hope you will rethink some of the things you say and realize the power of every word spoken.

Words are powerful, so why not use good, uplifting words instead of negative, abusive, and demeaning words? Taking this introspective look at yourself may not feel good, but I guarantee it will be well worth it, and you will be a better, more positive speaking person at the end of this journey. Throughout this book, I will share some of my experiences and challenges with how I've overcome them. You may be facing some of the same things. My desire is that my experiences will encourage you to do a deep dive into the hidden parts of yourself and make the necessary adjustments and become better. We are all striving to become a better version of ourselves, but it all begins within. Prepare your heart and mind for what will happen if you're willing to confront yourself.

What you say truly does shape you and the world around you.

3

What are You Saying?

Let's go back to your memories of the past, do you remember if your mom or dad said you were lazy? Did anyone ever say you were a problem child? Did you tell yourself that you had learning issues? Did you ever tell yourself that you couldn't do something because you weren't smart enough? Well, the fact is that some of these things may have been true to a certain degree, but do you think the more you were told you were lazy, that you took that as what you would always be? In essence, you would be what you were always called, lazy and unmotivated and so it became your reality. Did you ever think those words shaped you by what was being said? Do you do the same thing to others or yourself? What do you think of yourself? Are you attractive? Do you have a great sense of humor? How DO you see yourself? What do you think about yourself? I know these are some really difficult questions, but they need to be asked so that you can get to the core of why you are who you are.

I understand this will be a challenge, but don't worry, you will get through it. I took some time alone to answer these and many more questions about myself. I promise you, I didn't like the answers to many of these questions nor did I like what I saw when I looked into the mirror. What I saw and what I thought of myself was hard to face. I didn't want to face it, I only wanted to ignore it and hoped it would disappear. That was not going to happen, so I had to face the music and deal with the tune of self-reflection.

I told myself I wasn't good enough. I told myself I wasn't smart. I told myself that I would always be poor. I told myself that I would never amount to anything. Why did I have those thoughts about myself? After a lot of years, I finally had to face the "yuck" of me and what I kept telling myself. Since I told myself all those things, I *became* all of those things…over and over and over again.

My mom was always one to encourage me, however the one person I wanted to get encouragement and love from, but I never got. That person was my dad. He was not around to help my mom raise my siblings and me, and even though I wanted him to show me love, I never received it. For some reason, I took his not being there extremely personally. I don't know why I thought it was my fault, because it wasn't, but his not being there made me feel less than important and unloved. I went through much of my life with that empty hole of longing for a love I never received. Once I began to reflect on who I was and my choices, I traced those things back to what I felt inside. On the surface, no one knew what I was dealing with inside, probably because I learned at an early age to cover those things up. No one wants to deal with their feelings of loneliness, rejection, insecurity, low self-image, and low self-worth. These are issues we all deal with at some level, and it's time we talk about it and get free from those things that hold us in bondage.

We have only just begun this journey, but if you hang in there, you will find peace and freedom from the strings of those words that held you captive for years.

4

What are You Calling Yourself?

So, we've talked a bit about what others have said to you, now, let's address what you say to yourself. These can be words spoken or thoughts about who you are, what you are like, or even who you're not. I know this is a tough one because, as I mentioned, I had some pretty hard thoughts about myself. Let me take you further back into my world.

I am the middle of five, and you learn early on about what is called "middle child syndrome". When you search online, you'll find the "Middle child syndrome," which is the belief that a middle child is thought to be excluded, ignored, or even neglected because of their birth order. I am not saying this is true, but when the thought is placed in your mind, you tend to find reasons to make this true. Have you noticed this in your life? When you think about it, what do those who say these things know? It is just another label to put on us to turn us into what they want us to be. It's time to say enough is enough for those trying to mold you into their image. We were created in the image of God and should live accordingly [*Genesis 1:27 So God created man in his own image, in the image of God created he him; male and female created he*

7

them.]

This can be a hard pill to swallow, but it's necessary to overcome the overwhelming amount of negative words that come our way, not to mention the words we tell ourselves.

Here are a few examples of what I have heard people say about themselves:

- I'm stupid.
- I can't learn.
- I'm an idiot.
- No one loves me.
- People hate me.
- I'm boring.
- I'm not creative.
- I can't change; it's just the way I am.
- I'm too old to learn something new.
- I'm ugly, or I'm not pretty.
- I don't like the way I look.
- I'm too fat, I'm too skinny.
- I will always be alone.

This list can go on and on. I am sure you've heard someone say at least three of these things or you may have even said some of them about yourself. I know I have and I will be the first to admit it. One day, I realized that all of those things I was feeling about myself were only true because I thought about them or told them to myself enough that I began to believe it was true. Have you begun to believe all of the things that you have called yourself or what others may have called you? It is time to reverse all of those negative words to begin living a new life filled with powerfully positive words to combat all of the negative ones.

5

What Have You Allowed Others to Call You?

Taking the time to focus on what we say about ourselves versus what we allow others to say about us can be another hard reality to face. Especially considering who the person is that is throwing those negative words at you.. Is it someone you admire? Could it be someone you look up to? Are they a person of influence in your life? If so, this makes it even harder to discount what they may say to you. I can not say this has ever happened to me, but I understand how hard it is to free yourself from this situation. It took me many years to realize that I always wanted to please those in authority. My mom, my pastors, my teachers, my aunts and uncles, and those overseeing my life, I seek to be obedient and make sure they were pleased with what I did. Later on, I also realized that I needed to balance pleasing them and caring for myself. I always put others in front of myself; it was how I coped with my feelings of inadequacy. "Lift others, shine a light on them so no one will see me. Hide out in the background, maybe no one will notice me and bring attention to me." That was how I lived my life.

Words that could be spoken to you:

- You're a bum.
- You're lazy.
- Why aren't you more like your sister/brother?
- You will never amount to anything.
- You can't do anything right.
- Why were you even born?
- My life would be better off without you.
- You're so stupid.
- You're worthless.
- You're incompetent.
- You're an idiot.
- You're always late.
- You will never succeed.

We have heard this little saying and probably said it many times ourselves, "sticks and stones may break my bones, but words will never hurt me!" We didn't know it then, but that is the biggest lie ever told. I know we said it because everyone else said it, but the reality is those words hurt to the core! Some of those words we still remember and can't seem to let go of them. I know it took me many, many, many years to fight off some of the words said to me and even those I said to myself. I believe you will be successful on your journey to freedom as well.

6

What have you Thought About Yourself?

As we dig deeper into our thoughts about ourselves, it is important to be completely honest with how you think about yourself! When others say you are nothing and point out your character flaws, do you agree with them, or do you simply ignore what they're saying because you know what's true? How do you get over the negative words spoken to you? Do you replace them with positive ones that contradict what you've been told? I hope that is what you decide to do instead of agreeing with them. This is, of course, easier said than done and takes years of practice.

I have had some pretty horrible thoughts about myself, for more years than I should have. Once I decided to surround myself with people who would encourage me and tell me what they saw in me, I began to start seeing myself in a different light. I also had to pay attention to what I was listening to and what I was watching. Believe it or not, that plays a huge part in your attitude and how you feel in general. I am not going to tell you what you can and can not watch or listen to, but I had to make some major adjustments about what I allowed into my atmosphere. It was not easy, but if I wanted different, I had to choose

12

differently. I could not simply continue living and listening to hardcore music that was degrading women, arguing or fighting, cursing, and exuding anger if that's not what I wanted in my life. I needed to replace that with something uplifting, positive, and loving.

What did I use to base my new replacement verbiage on? The Word of God. This was an ongoing process, actually, it never stops. I must daily decide to choose positive instead of negative. Once I began to shift my circle of friends, my life shifted. It's not easy to let go of people, but I had to realize that sometimes people are in your life for a season and not always for a lifetime. You have to be strong enough to make the distinction and let go of those who may be hindering your progress. You must decide that you are more important and deserve to live a life opposite of the negative words spoken and thought about you. Shift the thoughts that you think about yourself.

New thoughts you can think about yourself:

- I am enough.
- I am loved.
- I am beautiful.
- I am handsome.
- I am happy.
- I am joyful.
- I am kind.
- I am a hard worker.
- I am valued.
- I am successful.
- I am smart.
- I am rich.
- I am friendly.

You may say that some of these things are not true, but were the words spoken earlier in your life true? No, they only became true when you started to take them as true, and you turned into those things. These phrases reverse what you were told and allow you to create a new thought that you can now begin working toward.

7

What is your Default, Positive or Negative?

I f I said to you, "you're a beautiful woman," or "you're a handsome man," is your initial thought, "you're right," or "you must be talking to someone else"? Most people who read this will be the former instead of the latter. Why is that? It is because of how we were brought up and what we have accepted as true all these years. I want to encourage you with this Psalm, it's one of my favorites. I am including the the bulk of chapter because there are so many good nuggets in it to leave out. Take a minute to read this and think about each word. I want you to feel as loved as I do after you read it.

This scripture is taken from The Passion Translation (TPT)

Psalms 139:1-18, 23-24 TPT *https://bible.com/bible/1849/psa.139.1-24.TPT*

"Lord, you know everything there is to know about me. You perceive every movement of my heart and soul, and you understand my every thought before it even enters my mind. You are so intimately aware of me, Lord. You read my heart like an open book and you know all the words I'm about to speak before I even start a sentence! You know every step I will take before my journey even begins. You've gone into my future to prepare the way, and in kindness

15

you follow behind me to spare me from the harm of my past. You have laid your hand on me! This is just too wonderful, deep, and incomprehensible! Your understanding of me brings me wonder and strength.

WOW! Let's stop right here and ponder what was just said. The Lord knows all there is to know about me. Everything! Every movement of my heart, my every thought, and He is intimately aware (having knowledge or perception) of me. Talk about someone paying serious attention to every detail of me. That makes me feel so loved, actually more loved than I could have ever imagined. Just think about someone knowing every word you are going to say before you even say them and every step before you take it. That last sentence before we move on, He not only has gone into my future but is also behind me to assure my past does not harm me. When I think about this, I think about the words that I thought about myself that were harmful. Instead of having a greater knowledge of this scripture, I allowed those words to become my reality instead of letting them go and refusing to believe them. Ok, let's keep reading.

Where could I go from your Spirit? Where could I run and hide from your face? If I go up to heaven, you're there! If I go down to the realm of the dead, you're there too! If I fly with wings into the shining dawn, you're there! If I fly into the radiant sunset, you're there waiting! Wherever I go, your hand will guide me; your strength will empower me. It's impossible to disappear from you or to ask the darkness to hide me, for your presence is everywhere, bringing light into my night. There is no such thing as darkness with you. The night, to you, is as bright as the day; there's no difference between the two.

There is nowhere I can go without Him being there! That blows my mind! Nowhere. That boggles my mind when I think about someone always with me wherever I go. If I'm alone, I'm not alone. When I feel like I can't find my way, there is always a path for me, even if I take the "wrong" one. He knows which one I'll take, and I will eventually end up where I was meant to be all along. How hard is it to fathom that kind of love? It's not something to try to figure out mentally, it will never happen!

15-18 You formed my innermost being, shaping my delicate inside and my intricate outside, and wove them all together in my mother's womb. I thank you, God, for making me so mysteriously complex! Everything you do is marvelously breathtaking. It simply amazes me to think about it! How thoroughly you know me, Lord! You even formed every bone in my body when you created me in the secret place; carefully, skillfully you shaped me from nothing to something. You saw who you created me to be before I became me! Before I'd ever seen the light of day, the number of days you planned for me were already recorded in your book. Every single moment you are thinking of me! How precious and wonderful to consider that you cherish me constantly in your every thought! O God, your desires toward me are more than the grains of sand on every shore! When I awake each morning, you're still with me.

Can you imagine being known before you were even conceived? What? This tells me that there was a plan for my life before I was given life. Every part of me was considered and laid out before my mom and dad knew about me. You have got to be getting excited about your life! You were not a mistake, even if your parents didn't plan on having you. The Lord had a plan, and you were conceived. He was thinking about you before you were you! It doesn't matter what anyone says about you, God Himself called you to be, and you were! I love how much He thinks of me and loves me with such an everlasting love. That love will never fade, change, or diminish, and it doesn't matter what I do, He continues to love and care for me.

23-24 God, I invite your searching gaze into my heart. Examine me through and through; find out everything that may be hidden within me. Put me to the test and sift through all my anxious cares. See if there is any path of pain I'm walking on, and lead me back to your glorious, everlasting way— the path that brings me back to you."

The Passion Translation® New Testament with Psalms, Proverbs, and Song of Songs, 2020 Edition

Published by BroadStreet Publishing® Group, LLC BroadStreetPublishing.com

ThePassionTranslation.com The Passion Translation® is a registered trademark of Passion & Fire Ministries, Inc.

Copyright © 2020 Passion & Fire Ministries, Inc. All rights reserved.

These last two verses are my response to ALL God has done for me in the previous verses. It is my asking Him to help me to continue to help me stay the course. This is a hard part because I'm offering Him to search my heart and point out where I may be wrong in my thinking and the words I might say to myself that are contrary to what He says about me. In my asking Him to search me, I have to be willing to be open and vulnerable with Him and be willing also to take His gentle prodding to clear out those incorrect thoughts and course-correct. His love for me is never ending, and I must forgive myself and change those negative words to positive ones.

I sincerely hope this scripture blessed you. I know it makes me think about a love like this, and I appreciate being loved so much that no matter where I go, God, the Father is there! I also love how there are moments in the chapter where King David asks the Lord to point out any anxious cares that he has as well as any path of pain he's walking on.

Doesn't that sound a lot like what we've been talking about? The pain of the words spoken to us and how hard it is to find a way of escape. Finding a path from negative to positive is not always easy, but you can make it out! Do you feel encouraged?

8

Where is the Silver Lining?

When you look at various situations in your life, how hard is it for you to find the silver lining? Do you automatically think the worst? Why do you think that is? Does that ever get on your nerves? Are your friends that way? It can be hard to nail down why we are the way we are, until we take a break from the busyness of life, sit down, and go back to locate when we started to dwell on the negative. Does it stem back to when you were a child? Does it go back to when you were in grade school, middle school, high school, or college? Was it your first job, your first boss, or your first co-worker? What about your first girlfriend or boyfriend? Your first crush? The list can keep going on and on, and truth be told, it could be a combination of many of these things that caused a negative spiral of emotions to overtake you and make you who you are today.

Once you pinpoint it, what are you going to do about it? This is not the time to say, "it's too late for me to change since I've been like this as long as I can remember!" If you take that route, you have learned nothing so far. The goal is to move from negative to positive. Negative thoughts and outlooks can make a person truly unlikable. After a while, no one wants to be around a person who is always negative. It's draining and depressing. If that is you, I hope you will consider adjusting your thoughts and words. Ask someone you are close to and trust to tell you the truth if you lean more toward negative or positive in your speech and thoughts. Only ask if you're ready to hear something other than what you think. More often than not, our thoughts are skewed and we could assume we are one way, yet we are completely the opposite. Happy asking!

Don't be discouraged in this process because it is just that…a process! It may have taken you many, many years to be the person you are, you can't expect it to change overnight magically. Give yourself the grace to grow and change. If you are a person who leans into a more positive mindset, befriend someone who is the opposite. They could use someone like you to help them do and be better, but you have to give them grace and time to change as well. We all need someone to help us grow to a better place. None of us are perfect and do all things right all the time. We are all in the process of doing better and being better. We have to decide daily to be a better version of ourselves today than we were yesterday.

9

Glass half empty or half full

Another determining factor about how you see things is whether you see a glass half empty or half full. Optimism versus Pessimism, of course, positive or negative. Why don't we look at the actual definitions of these words? Taken from the **American Heritage Dictionary of the English Language 5th Edition,** Optimism is defined as: A tendency to expect the best possible outcome or dwell on the most hopeful aspects of a situation. Pessimism is defined as: A tendency to stress the negative or unfavorable or to take the gloomiest possible view.

It is extremely interesting to see the initial definitions of those words. What stands out to me is something shortened like Favorable vs. Unfavorable and Hopeful aspects vs. Gloomiest view. Where do you find yourself? I desire to be on the side of favorable and hopeful. That is pretty much where I land more times than not.

Even in my space of having "not so happy feelings" about myself, I leaned more towards hopeful. As long as I can remember, I've always seen the glass as half full. I'm not sure where I got that from or why that has been the case. One of my sisters has always referred to me as the one who'd try to bring peace into a situation. I never liked arguments (and still don't) or any sort of fussing, disagreements, or bickering. I have always wanted people to get along. Is that too much to ask? I don't think so. In my mind, it was a pretty simple ask of those around me. I believe that when we were younger and didn't always have enough food or new clothes like other kids, I was taught to be grateful for what I did have. That is likely where the optimism comes in and how I felt. No matter what it looks like, it could be much worse. If we didn't like something my mom fixed us to eat, she would remind us that there were starving kids worldwide who didn't have food to eat. Of course, back then, we didn't care much about the starving kids and just knew we didn't want what she was serving us.

Have you heard people say, "There is always something," or "If it's not one thing, it's another"? Ever thought about those phrases? Ever wonder WHY they were always true? Probably because that's what they said and always said. Why would it be different if that's what is always said? You can't expect to get something other than what you continue to say. It seems so simple, but we always say things like that. How about this one, "my head is killing me." Really? This one bothers me more than anything, and when I hear people saying it, I ask them, "is it really killing you, though?" Once they think about it, they change it to say it's hurting. My question to them is, "what if you said that and you actually died?" There's no changing your words after that. I caution people about saying those things and pray that no one actually falls dead after saying something is killing them too much. Those words are extremely powerful, and we are all shaping our lives daily with what we say. We all have to work on adjusting our words to bring life, not death, positive and not negative.

10

Self Love, Self Care, Self Worth

know we touched on loving self earlier, but I feel like it needs its own section. I don't know about you, but loving myself for many years was hard. I didn't see my value in any area of my life, and at one point, I figured if I left this earth, no one would actually miss me. I know NOW that was a lie, but I didn't know it then. The crazy part is that no one knew I had those thoughts or feelings because I knew how to hide or mask what I was feeling. I laughed, smiled, and did all I needed to do around family and friends; however, inside I was hurting and alone.

I mentioned earlier that I desired to be loved by my dad, but I didn't tell you that since I didn't get the love I was searching for from my dad, I latched onto the first guy that showed me some attention. That led to a promiscuous lifestyle, an early marriage that led to divorce, and random relationships all searching for someone to love me more than I loved myself. I didn't know that I was going about things all wrong. I didn't know that I first needed to love myself for someone to love me. I hoped that if they loved me, it would "complete" the brokenness of who I was and fix that deep dark hole in my heart. None of that happened, but that didn't stop me from searching.

One day, many years later, I decided to cut off all the men I was dealing with and start spending some time with me! It was a hard decision, but I knew I needed to understand why I was so sad and empty. I had to take some time to search my life and get to know who I really was. One year for my birthday, I decided to take a trip to the beach by myself, get a room on the beach and just spend some time asking myself some hard questions. Who are you? What makes you tick? What do you love? Why don't you love yourself? Why have you moved from relationship to relationship? What are you looking for in a husband? What do you love about yourself? What do you dislike about yourself? Why are you here? These are some tough questions, but I wanted to really get to know myself. I had hidden my feelings for so long, I had to take some time to reintroduce myself to me. I cried many tears as I began getting to the root of those questions, but on the other side, I started this process of loving myself! I started taking myself out to dinner, to the movies, day trips, and anything I wanted to do because I didn't need someone to go with me. I was enough, and I truly began to enjoy my own company. I genuinely love who I am now because I know who I was and where I came from. It was a hard journey, but I knew it had to be taken.

Spending time to pamper yourself is a great way to care for yourself, get a manicure/pedicure, have a spa day, or have a little retail therapy. Any of the things that bring you joy do that. You must take time to care for yourself, especially if you are a person who cares for others more than you care for yourself. It was hard for me to do things for myself because I always ensured everyone else was taken care of. After I realized that I matter, I had to learn to say no to those asking me to do things so I could make time to do something for me! That was tremendously difficult for me since I was so used to doing everything for anyone who asked. I hated the feeling that I was letting someone down by telling them no, but I eventually found a balance between helping them and allowing time for me as well.

Making the time to pamper myself was hard, but what was harder was knowing my worth. I struggled for many years about being worthy of anything good! That is, sadly, something many of us deal with. Especially women. We often compare ourselves with other women. We think we should look a certain way to receive love and appreciation. We feel like if we were a particular size, we would automatically become more worthy of love and affection. Of course, none of these things are true, but that doesn't mean we don't feel that way. After I took the time to get to know who I was, I began to love myself. Reading and meditating on the Psalm that was shared earlier helped tremendously. Learning who I was in God's eyes helped me understand and appreciate how He made me. It didn't matter what I thought about myself, what actually mattered was what He thought about me, and eventually, those unworthy feelings about myself changed.

Along with those new feelings and a positive mindset about myself, came a joy that I had never experienced before. Happiness is one thing, but Joy is completely different. I realized that happiness is fleeting and comes and goes, but joy is a heart condition that lasts. Happy is defined as being content or having a feeling of contentment. Joy is defined as feeling great pleasure and having great delight. At the end of all of your searching, I desire that you find more than happiness; you will find joy and peace. You will not allow anyone or anything to interrupt that place once you find it. Protect it with all you have in you. Remember where you've come from and where you're going. Time for some action steps towards a better you.

11

Self Reflection

After all of the things we've talked about, now it's time for you to take some time to check your thoughts of you. What do you want to change about yourself?

Let's start by writing your negative thoughts about yourself, then write a positive to counteract those negative thoughts.

Negative thoughts of yourself	Positive thoughts of yourself

12

Affirmations

In the previous exercise, we wrote out the negative thoughts vs. positive ones to counteract the negative. Now it's time to take that a bit further. I did this while working on loving myself and getting away from those negative thoughts about me. I would look at myself in the mirror and tell myself that I am beautiful, I am loved, I am kind, I am appreciated, I am valued, I am loving, I am worthy, I am friendly, and the list would keep going. This is what I would like for you to do. This will help reverse all of the negative things said to yourself as well as those things you may have thought about yourself. If you were told you were lazy, you would write, I am a hard worker. If you were told you were dumb and would never amount to anything, you would write, I am smart, and I am successful. After you write these affirmations, you need to say them out loud. The more you say them, the more you rewire your brain to believe what you're saying. You will begin to notice a change in how you see yourself and, eventually how others see you. You will be more confident in what you're saying and who you are becoming based on the words spoken repeatedly.

Affirmations

13

Conclusion

I honestly hope that you have enjoyed this book. I desire that it has helped you with the words that you say and the words you allow others to say to you and about you. When we take the time to listen to what is being said with the knowledge of the power of words, we become more adamant about what's said and the effects of those words. Once you have read this book, consider sharing what you've learned with others. Share how important you realize words are and how they shape those around you. This journey starts with you. I was able to share all of my experiences because I took the time necessary to work on myself. It was not an easy process, but you can do it just like me. You will be overjoyed by the outcome if you are honest with yourself.

I would appreciate you leaving a review on Amazon if you have enjoyed this book and found it helpful. Please share with me your learning and successes.

Also by Gretta Berry

Photography Through the Lens of My Camera
How to See a Photo in Anything
Want to take your photography to the next level? Ever wanted some simple yet practical steps to taking better photos? Well, this book is for you!

This is a book about photography techniques and how to develop a photographer's eye for capturing images in everyday life. You will understand the importance of seeing potential photo opportunities in everyday objects and environments. You will be provided with tips and tricks for how to make the most out of those opportunities to create visually interesting photographs.

What you will discover in this book;
   Unique perspective
   Inspiring examples
   Action steps to improve
   Practical advice
   Training your eye

This book takes you directly to the heart of photography and shows you can take your photos from good to great. If you're ready to take the journey with me to seeing a photo in anything, grab your phone, your point-and-shoot or DSLR and let's explore together.

There is no need to feel intimated about photography, because in this small easy to understand book we explore and experience the simple tools needed to be successful and shoot more appealing photos than ever before.